Some words you will find in this book:

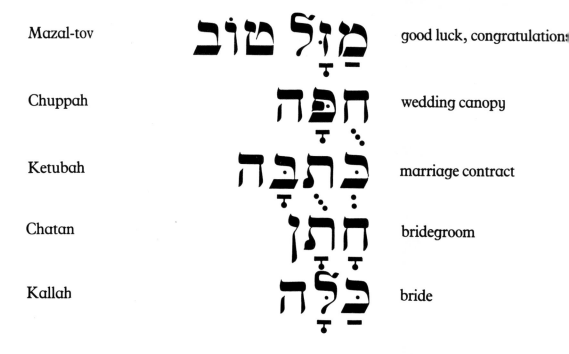

Mazal-tov	מַזָּל טוֹב	good luck, congratulations
Chuppah	חֻפָּה	wedding canopy
Ketubah	כְּתֻבָּה	marriage contract
Chatan	חָתָן	bridegroom
Kallah	כַּלָּה	bride

Some of the scenes in this book have been re-enacted to comply with Jewish tradition.

The author and publishers would like to thank the following: Rabbi and Mrs. C. Ingram, Karen and Gary Marks, the Nyman family, Richard Reggal and Ron May. Without their understanding and co-operation this book could not have been written.

The photograph on page 7 of a 17th-century Italian Ketubah is reproduced with the permission of the Jewish Museum, London.

MAZAL-TOV
A JEWISH WEDDING

José Patterson

Photographs by Liba Taylor

Hamish Hamilton   London

מַזְּל טוֹב
Mazal-tov

Congratulations to Gary and Karen who are getting married. These two Hebrew words mean 'good luck' and are used as a special greeting for all happy Jewish occasions, especially weddings.

Gary is manager of a wine shop in Glasgow. Although Karen has worked as a secretary and a model she has always loved to dance. She wants to become a dancing teacher when she is married.

Karen's mother and her sister Elaine enjoy helping her to open the wedding cards from friends and relations. They all contain the greeting 'mazal-tov', as well as good wishes for their future happiness.

Karen and Gary have been given lots of wedding presents. One is a special gift called a Mezuzah. This is a small case containing a tiny parchment scroll. There are holy verses written on the scroll. The verses are part of a daily prayer.

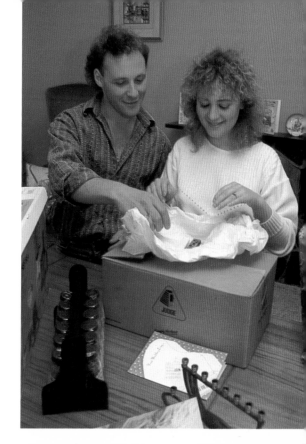

Karen and Gary will put the Mezuzah on the doorpost of their new home as a sign of God's presence. This Mezuzah belongs to Karen's parents. The Hebrew letters on it stand for 'Almighty God'.

This is Gary's cousin Richard who is nine years old. Boxing is Richard's favourite sport. Every time Gary comes to stay he gives Richard some coaching. 'You'll have to watch your left hook,' Gary explains.

Richard lives next door to Karen. It was when Gary came to stay with Richard that he first met Karen. 'I'm glad they met in my house,' says Richard. 'Karen will soon be my cousin too.'

Although Karen and Gary made their own plans to marry, Jewish marriages used to be arranged by a marriage-maker called a Shadchan. A few Jewish marriages are still arranged today.

The Shadchan would speak to the parents about wedding plans for their children. The couple would meet only when the marriage was agreed.

Karen has asked Richard to be her page boy. He is very pleased and shows Gary the kipah he will wear at the wedding. All Jewish men and boys wear a kipah in the Synagogue. It is a sign of respect for God.

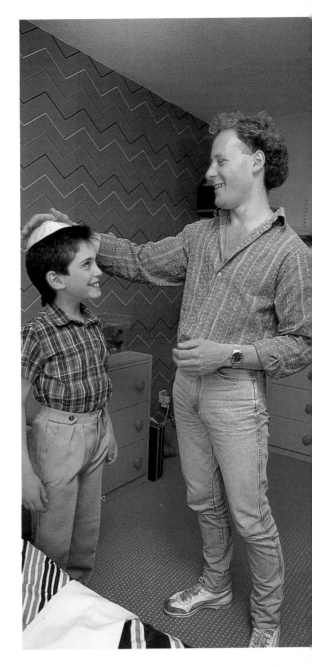

Before their wedding Karen and Gary talk to Rabbi Ingram who is the Minister of the Synagogue. He explains the meaning of the Ketubah, the Jewish marriage contract.

Karen and Gary will both sign the Ketubah using their Hebrew names. They must understand everything it says.

Rabbi Ingram explains the promises that the Chatan, Jewish bridegroom, makes to the Kallah, his bride:

'I will work for you, honour, support and keep you as is the custom of Jewish husbands.'

A Ketubah can be bought ready prepared, but some are hand written by Jewish scribes. They are trained to write Hebrew with a special pen made from a goose feather.

This beautifully decorated Ketubah is over 300 years old. Can you see the Hebrew words 'mazal-tov' in the bottom corners?

A few days before her wedding Karen comes to this special ritual bath called a Mikveh. She says a short prayer to God. When she has been under the water Karen is cleansed and pure for her wedding. This special bath marks a fresh start in her life.

When the wedding day arrives, everyone is busy and excited. Karen goes into the garden to show her wedding dress to her father. He admires the delicate material and the beautiful embroidery. He is very proud of his daughter today.

Elaine is Karen's bridesmaid and wears a lovely pink dress. Richard is very smart in his pink bow tie and sash. He is a helpful pageboy and makes sure Elaine's bow is straight.

Before the wedding the photographer comes to take some pictures of Karen and her family. Everyone is so happy he does not need to remind them to smile!

Next door Richard is taking a photograph of the bridegroom. 'I'll put this picture of you on the first page of my album,' he says.

Now it time for Karen to set off for the Synagogue. Her dress and veil are so long she has to be helped into the car. 'Be careful they don't get trapped in the door,' she tells her mother.

The wedding guests stand outside the Synagogue and chat to each other. They exchange the special greeting 'mazal-tov'. Can you see the Hebrew words above the entrance to the Synagogue? They come from the bible.

Gary's friend Mike is the best man. 'I hope Gary is not going to be late,' he says. Karen's brother Andy suggests they all go inside to wait for the bridegroom.

One of the wedding cars arrives. Richard holds Elaine's bag while she steps out.

13

Karen enters the Synagogue by a side door. She will not go to the main part of the Synagogue yet.

Mrs Ingram the Rabbi's wife and Karen's mother chat to her while she waits. They tell her what a beautiful bride she looks.

14

When Gary arrives he says a special prayer before he puts on his talit – a prayer shawl. Gary stands between his father and Karen's father to say some prayers. The proud grandparents are waiting for the ceremony to begin.

When the prayers are over Rabbi Ingram takes Gary to see his bride. Gary performs the 'bedecken' ceremony. This is an old custom in which the bridegroom covers the bride's face with a veil. He says a few lines from the Bible.

Karen's father proudly takes Karen into the Synagogue to
stand under the Chupah – the bridal canopy. The Chupah is
supported on four poles and decorated with ribbons and
flowers. It stands in front of the Holy Ark. This is a place
where the Torah Scrolls of the holy scriptures are kept. The
Ark faces east in the direction of Jerusalem.

The congregation stand and listen as Rabbi Ingram sings hymns of praise to God. Everyone enjoys listening to his beautiful voice. He prays that God may bless the Chatan and Kallah. The Rabbi tells them that their love for each other should equal their love of God and the Jewish people.

He hopes they will take after their parents in making the Sabbath a holy day and keeping a kosher home. To keep a kosher home Jewish people must follow special rules about what they eat. The food which is allowed is called kosher food.

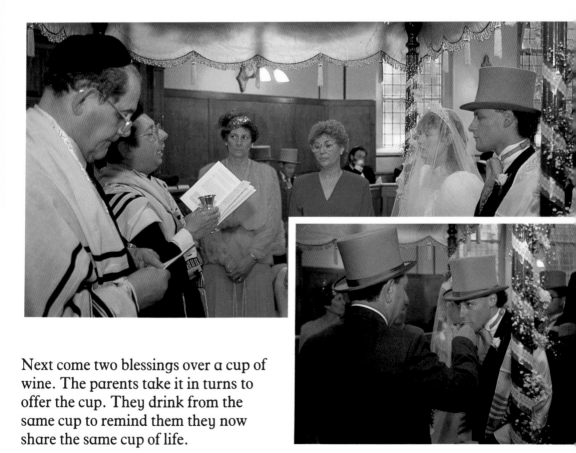

Next come two blessings over a cup of wine. The parents take it in turns to offer the cup. They drink from the same cup to remind them they now share the same cup of life.

This is the most solemn part of the wedding service. The bridegroom places a ring on the first finger of the bride's right hand and slowly repeats the ancient blessing after the Rabbi:

'This ring makes our marriage sacred, according to the Law of Moses and Israel.'

The ceremony ends with the singing of the Seven Marriage Blessings. Lastly Gary stamps on a glass and smashes it. This custom is a reminder of the sadness all Jews feel at the destruction of their Temple in Jerusalem nearly 2000 years ago.

After the ceremony is over, the bridal pair walk to the Bimah – the raised platform – to sign their documents.

'We'll start off in the right way – you sign first,' says Gary to Karen. The young couple are now married.

'I'll have to get used to being called Mrs Marks,' says Karen happily.

Later on the guests go to the Synagogue hall to greet the bride and groom and enjoy a drink and a snack. Richard offers some food to his mother, grandmother and brother Jamie.

Before the wedding feast begins, Rabbi Ingram says a blessing for the bread. This plaited loaf is called challah and is eaten on the Sabbath day and festivals. An extra large loaf is needed to supply all the guests.

After the meal Richard takes a picture of Karen and Gary with their little good luck teddy bear. 'This one will have a very special place in my album,' he says.

Karen's father thanks the families and friends for taking part in their 'simcha' – a joyful celebration. He welcomes his new son-in-law into the family. He is sure Gary will make a good husband and a caring father for their future children.

Karen gives her father a big thank-you kiss. She knows how hard her parents have worked to make sure the wedding is a success.

Everyone raises their glasses and joins
Gary's parents in wishing the
newlyweds the Hebrew toast
'le Chaim' – to Life.

Slowly and carefully the first cut is
made in the wedding cake. Everyone
will have a slice. Richard will have
some extra pieces to give to his school
friends.

When the delicious meal is over, it is time for music and dancing. Everyone claps their hands to the rhythm of a Russian dance. Gary and his friends kick out their legs from a squatting position. Although they make it look easy, it is very difficult to do.

The guests clap and cheer as Karen and Gary dance together.

A Jewish bride and groom are regarded as king and queen on their thrones. Karen and Gary are seated on chairs and lifted up and carried round by their friends.

The bride and groom are leaving. Karen thanks Richard for being a splendid page boy. Richard gives her a big kiss.

'I'd like to be a page boy again!' he says. 'I wonder when Elaine plans to get married?'

HAMISH HAMILTON CHILDREN'S BOOKS

Penguin Books Ltd, 27 Wrights Lane, London W8 5TZ (Publishing & Editorial)
and Harmondsworth, Middlesex, England (Distribution & Warehouse)
Viking Penguin Inc., 40 West 23rd Street, New York, New York 10010, U.S.A.
Penguin Books Australia Ltd, Ringwood, Victoria, Australia
Penguin Books Canada Limited, 2801 John Street, Markham, Ontario, Canada L3R 1B4
Penguin Books (N.Z.) Ltd, 182–190 Wairau Road, Auckland 10, New Zealand

First published in Great Britain 1988 by
Hamish Hamilton Children's Books
Design by Tony Garrett
Copyright © 1988 (text) by José Patterson
Copyright © 1988 (photographs) by Liba Taylor

British Library Cataloguing-in-Publication Data:
Patterson, José
Mazal-tov: a Jewish wedding.
1. Marriage customs and rites, Jewish –
Juvenile literature
I. Title
392'.5'088296   BM713

ISBN 0–241–12269–4

Printed in Great Britain by
Cambus Litho Ltd. East Kilbride